Tales of
TWO
FRANKS

40 MIRACULOUS
DELIVERANCE TESTIMONIES!

FRANK HAMMOND & FRANK MARZULLO

THE TALES OF TWO FRANKS

as told by

FRANK HAMMOND & FRANK MARZULLO

ISBN 10: 0-89228-066-2
ISBN 13: 978-089228-066-7

IMPACT CHRISTIAN BOOKS, INC.

332 Leffingwell Ave., Suite 101
Kirkwood, MO 63122

WWW.IMPACTCHRISTIANBOOKS.COM

For a full list of Impact's titles, refer to the website above or use your camera with the **QR Code**

PREFACE

FRANK MARZULLO and FRANK HAMMOND became life-long friends and fellow deliverance ministers after they first met and ministered together at the Tennessee-Georgia Christian Camps in 1975. They traveled together with their wives to various cities in the United States, Mexico, England and Columbia.

Over the years they shared with one another the humorous, strange, exciting and bizarre things experienced in their ministries of healing and deliverance.

In *The Tales of Two Franks* they tell some of their most memorable experiences. You will appreciate the frankness of these two Franks as they admit mistakes and failures along with amazing victories and unexpected happenings.

The two Franks are transparent, giving you an insight into their private lives that shows their love of God, love for people and enjoyment of the ministry to which God has called them.

This is an easy-to-read and enjoyable book that not only contains interesting tales but discloses valuable truths.

Part I

the Tales of Frank Hammond

THE DEVIL WINS ROUND ONE

When Ida Mae and I first became aware of deliverance, we lived in the small town of Frisco, Colorado where I was pastor of a small fellowship in our home. We had no mentors, no resource materials and no experience; it was a mixture of ignorance and inexperience, and a recipe for excitement, failure and learning.

One evening I returned home from a trip to find Ida Mae and several other ladies attempting to cast demons out of a very unstable woman in our community. If anyone could have demons we believed she qualified. As pastor, I was immediately drawn into the attempted deliverance. I call it "attempted" because that's all it was.

As soon as a demon was addressed it would surface and speak through the woman. One demon who spoke through her declared, "If Jesus were here I would have to leave, but He is not here." As each of us stood in shock, one of our dear ladies fell on her face and beating the carpet with her fists began shouting, "Come back, Jesus! Don't leave us Jesus! We need you, Jesus!"

It took awhile for us to analyze the demon's assertion that Jesus had deserted us. By the time we concluded that the demon was lying, he spoke again, "There is just one of you here that is really following the Lord, the rest of you are just tagging along." Each of us thought, "No wonder we are not getting anywhere with this deliverance. No one besides me is really following the Lord." We were hopelessly divided.

The demon was so successful in ministering confusion and distrust of one another that nothing was accomplished. Not one demon was cast out that night.

When new recruits in God's army engage the enemy for the first time, he will do everything he can to discourage and defeat them so that they will back off from deliverance. Thank God, we had tenacity, and refused to give up because of this initial failure. It took awhile for us to find true team unity, but we finally did. We also grew in boldness of faith. We became convinced that the devil and demons are all liars, and that we have authority over them. We lost one battle, but we were determined not to lose the war.

DEMON BLACKENS IDA MAE'S EYES

God chose Ida Mae to be the first one in our fellowship to receive deliverance. We had invited Andy Smith as a guest teacher. He paused in his teaching and announced, "Someone here has a *spirit of torment*, and I can't go on until it is dealt with."

None of us were accustomed to putting names on our problems. Finally, Ida Mae cautiously lifted her hand and said, "Sir, I think it might be me." Ida Mae realized that she was tormented over our teen-aged-daughter, Joyce, being out on snowy mountain highways at night making school trips to ball games.

Andy put one hand on Ida Mae's shoulder and commanded, "You *demon of torment* come out of her!" Down she went with the demon speaking through her. She dug her fingers into the thick pile carpet and actually lifted it several inches off the floor! After torment was cast out another spirit surfaced — a *spirit of high blood pressure*. Ida Mae had almost died of uremic poisoning when our daughter was born. The doctor had predicted that Ida would have high blood pressure by the time she was forty. She was right on schedule! A doctor had recently informed her that her blood pressure was high.

When Andy commanded the *spirit of high blood pressure* to come out, the demon caused her head to swell so extremely that blood vessels around her eyes ruptured. The demon had torn her just as we read about in the ministry of Jesus (see MARK 1:26; 9:20).

The next morning Ida Mall's eyes were still black and blue (I took a snapshot of her which I still have). She could not go to work as a bank employee for two days. The third day she put on heavy makeup and returned to work. Her fellow employees wanted to know why she missed work. Ida Mae told them, "I had an intruder in my house, and he resisted when we tried to put him out." They just laughed, and didn't ask any more questions.

Our church members had never seen anything like this, so everyone left the meeting in awe over what the pastor's wife had experienced. When they came back on Sunday, Ida Mae stood up and said, "I know you are wondering about what happened to me Wednesday night. I have a peace that I've never experienced before. I heartily recommend deliverance."

DEMONS MATERIALIZE

Soon after our first book, *Pigs in the Parlor*, was published, we were invited to be interviewed on a Christian television network. When we arrived at the studio, to our dismay a new program director was in charge who did not believe a Christian could have a demon. We were forbidden to talk about deliverance, and the program director crouched beneath the camera and glared at us to make sure that we didn't mention deliverance on the air. We were very disappointed at this turn of events and felt that our trip was in vain. God had other plans for us.

On our way out of the studio one of the secretaries stopped us, and, knowing that we were deliverance ministers, requested ministry. We invited her to our motel room. A waste basket was set in front of her and a box of facial tissues was nearby just in case they were needed.

A spirit of abortion was discerned. "Have you had an abortion?" Ida Mae asked. "Yes, in fact I've had three," she replied. We explained that abortion is murder, so we would call out the companion *spirits of abortion and murder*. We then led her in a prayer of confession and repentance, asking the Lord's forgiveness.

When we commanded the *demons of abortion and murder* to go in the name of Jesus, her neck swelled so severely that tiny blood capillaries began to rupture on her neck and lower face. She was choking and unable to breathe. A few seconds seemed like eternity as we kept commanding the demons to leave. Suddenly, something large flew out of her mouth and fell in the waste basket. All three of our heads went over the basket to see what it was. To our amazement there was a blob of fresh red blood about the size of a silver dollar, and next to it lay a perfectly formed embryo about three inches long. The lady questioned, "Do you see what I see?" We tried not to act surprised. "That didn't come from my stomach," she explained. "I haven't had anything to eat for seven hours." "No, it formed in your throat," we assured her.

The demons had materialized! The clot of fresh blood represented the spirit of murder. The embryo was the spirit of abortion.

When Ida emptied the embryo in the toilet, she moved it around in the water to examine it closely. Without question, it was a perfectly formed fleshly embryo.

By questioning the woman, we learned that she and her family had been very involved in *spiritism* where the materialization of spirits is encouraged. We concluded that this connection with spiritism explained why these particular demons materialized. Deliverance ministers never lack for challenges and surprises!

All who have, who perform, who assist with, or who agree with abortion, are guilty of murder. Deliverance awaits all sinners who repent and accept God's forgiveness.

WRONG CHOICE OF WORDS

I'd like to share a humorous thing that happened when I used a poor choice of words. My brother-in-law, Willard, and I were ministering to a sweet little lady who was a children's worker in a church I had previously pastored. The deliverance was going quite well until I discerned a spirit of sexual lust. I commanded, "You spirit of lust come out of her." The spirit caused her to reach out her hands and stroke my arms seductively. I commanded, "Get your hands off of me, you filthy demon." Her hands jerked back momentarily, and then they began to grope for my arms again. After rebuking the lust spirit three times, it began to grope for Willard (all this time the sister's eyes were shut). In a syrupy drawl the demon exclaimed, "Oh, Willard, you are so attractive!" Whereupon, I countered, "Shut up, you lying spirit." Willard looked at me with a surprised expression on his face and with feigned indignity declared, "I'm changing sides!"

AUTHOR'S NOTE: The spirit of sexual lust had gained entrance into her through fantasy lust: fantasizing herself in relationship with men other than her husband.

FALSE PREGNANCY

We were leading a deliverance seminar in New Orleans, Louisiana. A lady and her husband came to us at the end of the first service. She appeared large with child. "When is your baby due!" Ida Mae inquired. "I've been pregnant for twelve months," she explained. "Every day I spend hours confessing life into the child. After our last child was born, we decided we didn't want any more children, so my husband had a vasectomy. Then we decided that this was wrong, so by faith we claimed that the vasectomy had been reversed, and by faith I became pregnant."

Now, this was a church whose pastor became a devoted follower of a prominent faith teacher who had drifted into error. Her pastor had led his people into an imbalanced faith walk. The entire church was caught up in the woman's prolonged pregnancy. They were puzzled and confused but unwilling to face the possibility that anything was amiss. She felt no movement of the baby in her body, so everyone in the fellowship was praying for life in the womb.

Ida Mae, who was very accurate in *words of knowledge* and *discerning of spirits*, said, "You have a false pregnancy." Tactfully and gently we lead the lady and her husband to renounce the false pregnancy and command the spirit to leave. A group of people had gathered around us to observe how we would minister.

At the following night's service, the woman immediately sought us out. Her abdomen was completely flat, and she was not wearing a maternity dress! The pregnancy was false and demonic. We recalled the scripture, "We have been with child, we have been in pain; We have, as it were, brought forth wind" (Isa. 26:18).

Can faith in God reverse a vasectomy? Of course! Nothing is impossible with God. Can faith in God bring forth a child to a woman whose husband is impotent? Yes, indeed! All things are possible to them that believe.[1] The problem here was that this couple had not grown in faith but felt obligated to maintain a posture of faith in order to be accepted by the pastor and congregation of which they were a part. Their so-called faith was mere presumption.

This couple was totally relieved that the charade was over, and so was the pastor and the whole church. To show their appreciation, the couple showered us with presents. Even after we left they mailed us other gifts.

Deception is a powerful trap that the devil employs to lead us into

---

1 See *Deliverance from Childlessness* by Bill Banks for numerous cases of infertility being healed. Available at **www.impactchristianbooks.com/banks**

error and shipwreck our faith. No wonder we need *words of knowledge* and the *discerning of spirits*. We must also speak the truth in love to those snared in Satan's deceptions.

SWINE IN THE KITCHEN

Pastor John Edwards from Croydon, England, was traveling from England to Poland by car. He was crossing the Czechoslovakian border. This was in the 1980's during the Communist regime. In his luggage he carried a copy of our book, *Pigs in the Parlor*. To the Communist border guards, any kind of literature was suspect, especially religious material. The border guard found the book and demanded to know what it was. John didn't know how to speak Czech, and the guard didn't know English but knew German. John knew a little German, so they attempted to communicate in German. John came up with the German word for "swine," but he didn't know the word for "parlor," so he substituted the word for "kitchen." "Swine in the Kitchen," John replied in German. The border guard responded in German, "Oh, cook book. No problem."

So, *Pigs in the Parlor* became known as a cook book; instructions for roasting the devil's hide!

MINISTERING ANGELS

My wife and I became very aware of angels assigned to protect us when we traveled. On several occasions, people in our meetings reported seeing us surrounded by angels. We believe they were there to protect us.

> Are they [angels] not all ministering spirits sent forth to minister for those who inherit salvation?
>
> HEB. 1:14

There were many times when we could have been killed or severely injured but were miraculously spared. One such occasion happened in

Boston. We were in a car with a pastor and his wife traveling through the downtown area. We two men were in the front seat and our wives in the back. It was a rainy day. While going through an intersection on a green light, suddenly, from our left, a car ran a red light and came hurtling towards us at high speed. We braced for the inevitable crash! Someone shouted, "Jesus!" The other car passed through the front of ours as a shadow. We were so stunned that we sat in silent shock for several minutes before anyone could speak. We four eye-witnesses agreed, the other car *actually* passed through the engine of our vehicle as a harmless shadow.

> "For He shall give His angels charge over you, To keep you in all your ways"
>
> PSALM 91:11

PRIDE GOES BEFORE A FALL

We were ministering to a twenty-year-old man. A spirit had surfaced, and I commanded, "What is your name?" He replied, "I be the *spirit of pride*" (this was at a time before the Lord instructed us not to converse with demons). "What kind of pride do you promote?" I inquired. The spirit boasted, "All pride come through me." The spirit was talking like an Indian chief. All the while the *pride spirit* was causing the young man to lift his head in a gesture of pride and tilt his chair slowly backward. Suddenly, the chair toppled backward, and the man crashed onto the floor.

We had just witnessed a literal fulfillment of PROVERBS 16:18, *"Pride goes before destruction, and a haughty spirit before a fall."*

PUFFED UP WITH PRIDE

At another time we encountered a spirit of pride in a fourteen year old boy, a preacher's son. The spirit manifested by expanding the boy's chest abnormally. There is no way that he could have puffed out his chest like that. It was altogether supernatural. His appearance reminded us of lizard when it puffs his throat like a balloon.

Paul said to some of the Corinthians, "*You are puffed up, and have not rather mourned*" (1 COR. 5:2). Again, "*learn in us not to think of men above that which is written, that no one of you be puffed* [Greek **phusioo**, to be puffed up with pride] *up for one against another*" (1 COR. 4:6B).

Satan and his demons, by nature, are prideful. They will try to occupy center stage, so to speak, even when they are on the threshold of being cast out. They are filled with empty boasting.

During the deliverance of a certain man, demons began to speak through him and boasted, "I'm stronger than you. You will never be able to cast me out. You will get tired and have to go to bed, but I'll still be here. I will be as strong as ever." I replied something like this, "You are nothing but a puny demon. The blood of Jesus is powerful against you. I command you to leave in Jesus' Name!" "But where will I go?" the prideful demon whined as he left.

Where did the demon go? Jesus taught, "*when the unclean spirit goes out of a man, it passes through waterless places seeking rest, and does not find it*" (MATT. 12:43, NASB). All their boasting and braggadocio is in vain. Jesus has said,

> "Behold, I have given you authority to tread on serpents and scorpions, and over all the power of the enemy, and nothing will injure you."
>
> LUKE 10:19, NASB

DEMONS ADMIT TO POWER IN THE BLOOD

"And they overcame him by the blood of the lamb."
REV. 12:11

We had been casting out demons only a short time before we discovered the awesome power of the blood of Jesus to terrorize and defeat demons.

Libbie, our daughter-in-law, was very teachable and hungry for the things of God. When we shared deliverance truth with her, she was ready to receive. As we began to command tormenting demons, they threw her to the floor. As I knelt beside her writhing body, I reminded the demons of the power of the blood. The demon being addressed cried out in a loud voice, "Don't talk about the blood of Jesus. I can't stand it! It has power that we don't have. It is so red, so warm, so alive! It just covers everything."

We don't get our theology from demons, for we know their proneness to lie; nevertheless, when demons are faced with the Anointed One and the power of His blood they are apt to cry out in confession of Truth, as one did when confronted by Jesus Himself. The demon cried out,

> "Let us alone; what have we to do with thee, thou Jesus of Nazareth? art thou come to destroy us? I know thee who thou art, the Holy One of God."
>
> MARK 1:24

Afterward, we asked our daughter-in-law to tell us what she was experiencing during the deliverance. She could hear the demon speaking through her, but at the same time her spirit was in perfect peace. She said, "Big dad (as she called me), I saw such love in your eyes. I saw the love of Jesus in your eyes."

What a lesson! When we minister deliverance, we bring terror and defeat to the demons, and at the same time we minister the love and peace of Jesus to the ones being set free.

THE BLOOD OF JESUS CAUSES DEMONS TO PANIC

Another "power in the blood" experience happened while we were leading a deliverance seminar in Florida. We had concluded the praise service with Ida Mae teaching a new chorus on the blood of Jesus. I began my message by teaching the people to use the blood of Jesus as a weapon; telling demons what the blood of Jesus does: it redeems, justifies, sanctifies, cleanses and atones for our sins.

At this point, a woman in the fifth row of seats stood up, and pointing her finger at me, shouted, "Frank Hammond, you shut up!"

She sat back down with a puzzled expression on her face. When I started to teach again she stood up a second time and yelled, "Frank Hammond, I said for you to shut up!" Recognizing that a demon was speaking through the woman, I bound him in the name of Jesus and told him to remain quiet until I finished teaching. At the time for ministry, the demon was cast out.

Years later, we received a letter from the lady who identified herself by the disturbance she had created (actually, it was the demon and not the lady who cried out). She said the demon hated the chorus and the teaching on the blood of Jesus.

BREAKING VOODOO CURSES LEADS TO HEALING

The church in Phoenix, Arizona, that invited us to minister met in a store-front building. Prior to the service, I was in the process of unloading several boxes of books and tapes from our van when a man on crutches came up the sidewalk. He wanted to know where the deliverance service would be held and where he could find Frank Hammond. I said, "I'm Frank."

The man said that he was parked in his motor home, praying and listening to his radio when he heard our deliverance meeting announced. He explained, "The Lord told me that if I would attend this meeting and have Frank Hammond pray for me, I would be healed."

He identified himself as a missionary evangelist affiliated with a denomination that insists a Christian cannot have a demon. "Even though I believe that way, I'm here because the Lord told me to come," he explained.

I invited the minister to come inside, and we went into the pastor's study for prayer. He explained the crutches. He had fallen off a ladder onto a concrete driveway and shattered the bones in his ankle. He had been through a long medical procedure involving surgery, six weeks in a cast and severe pain. He was still in great pain, and doctors told him there was nothing more they could do. Prior to the ladder accident he had been injured in a private plane crash and other accidents. He was depressed because he was no longer able to travel and minister.

The Holy Spirit gave me discernment that he was under a curse, and I asked him if he had ever been involved in the occult. He explained that he had been on a ministry trip to Haiti and decided to attend a voodoo meeting to learn what they did and to take pictures. He took pictures of a voodoo man killing a rooster, and he watched as a man, under the power of demons, ate most of a thick, glass tumbler. He was handed the remains of the tumbler as a souvenir. Afterward he showed the pictures and the tumbler to churches where he ministered.

I said, "You are under a curse, and these accidents are happening because you attended that voodoo ceremony." He agreed to ask the Lord's forgiveness and to destroy the pictures and the tumbler as soon as he got home. When I commanded the *spirits of voodoo* to come out of him, he gagged and wretched as the demons left him.

Suddenly, he leaped to his feet and began to jump up and down. "I'm healed!" he shouted. "All the pain is gone!"

I asked the brother to testify in the service that evening, and he stood beside me at the altar call, assisting with deliverance and healing. He left without his crutches; completely healed. Glory to God!

POLISH DEMON SPEAKS ENGLISH

We were ministering at a youth camp in Wisla, Poland. The other teachers were John Edwards and Robert Ferguson from England. Five young men arrived a day late for the conference, just in time for noon lunch. We arranged for them to sit at our table with an interpreter. None of these men spoke any English and none of us knew any Polish.

As the five shared their need for deliverance, it was decided that we should minister to them right then and there. While the deliverance was progressing, one of the young men slid like an eel out of his chair and under the table. Robert crawled under the table, continuing to command the demons to come out. Suddenly, Robert stuck his head up from under the table and excitedly exclaimed in his English accent, "This bloke is cursing me in English!" The youth did not know one word of English, but the demon in him did!

His Seminary Taught False Doctrine

In 1975, a year after *Pigs in the Parlor* was published, Ida Mae and I were invited to teach deliverance at the Greater Pittsburgh Charismatic Conference, meeting on the campus of Duquesne University. The attendance topped eight thousand at the evening services, and Ida Mae and I were asked to serve as counselors for those responding to the altar call of salvation, baptism in the Holy Spirit, healing and deliverance.

The last person waiting for ministry was wearing a clerical collar. He was an Episcopal priest. He stated that another counselor had referred him to us for the kind of help he needed. After he had explained what he wanted God to do for him, we told him that he needed deliverance. He wasn't at all familiar with deliverance. We told him plainly that we would expel demons. He protested, "I don't believe in demons. I went to seminary, and they taught that when Jesus talked about demons He was merely accommodating himself to what the people believed."

We suggested that he allow us to address demons. If there were none in him then nothing would happen, but if any demons were in him they would come out. He was so desperate for help that he agreed to our proposal.

When the first demon was challenged, the priest was instantly seized by the spirits. He couldn't move, his legs, his arms or even speak. He appeared and acted like he had a severe case of spastic paralysis. About this time an announcement came over the public address system, "This building must be vacated immediately. Anyone not out of this building in five minutes will be locked up overnight. I repeat, this building must be vacated immediately."

Since the priest couldn't walk, we enlisted a couple of men to help us get him out of the building and across campus to the high rise dormitory where we were staying. A campus guard eyed us dragging him across the street, but he didn't ask any questions or interfere. He probably thought the poor guy was dead drunk. Finally, we got him on the elevator and up to our room on the seventh floor.

Over the next two hours he received a massive deliverance. Finally, he was free! He inquired, "What time is it?" It was 1:00 a.m. He exclaimed, "I must go! I have to be at my church by nine o'clock, and it's about an eight hour trip. I scarcely have time to get there. But I know what I'm going to tell my people. I've learned two things at this conference; I've learned how real Jesus is, and I've learned how real the devil is, and that's what I'm going to tell them!"

DIVINE PROTECTION FROM MURDEROUS SPIRIT

The next year, we were teaching again at the Greater Pittsburgh Charismatic Conference. Our meeting place was a theater in the basement of an old church. It was packed with about five hundred people. There was not one empty seat, so several people were standing in the back of the auditorium.

While I was teaching in preparation for deliverance, a disturbance started in the back of the room. From the platform it looked like a man was waltzing with a twelve foot stepladder. The ladder was tilting first one direction and then another. Finally, the ladder crashed into the last two rows of seats — the only four empty seats in the room! The people sitting in those seats had for one reason or another vacated them moments before.

I was continuing to teach, but almost everyone's attention was on the disturbance in the rear of the auditorium. Ida Mae rushed back to see what was going on. The man who had caused the disturbance was under the control of demons and writhing on the floor. A dozen people had thrown their Bibles on top of him. Ida Mae, and a couple other composed individuals, began to cast the demons out.

When the demons were out, the man had a very interesting story. He said that a demon was telling him to go up on the platform and kill Frank Hammond. He was trying to get to me and kill me when he got tangled in the stepladder!

God had protected me just as He promised,

> "Behold, I give unto you power to tread on serpents and scorpions, and over all the power of the enemy: and nothing shall by any means hurt you."
>
> LUKE 10:19

By the way, don't attempt to defeat the devil by throwing Bibles at him, "*The weapons of our warfare are not carnal*" (2 COR. 10:4). Follow the example of Jesus by quoting the Word to the devil saying; "*It is written...*" (MATT. 4:4).

MEET MR. ITCH

After the Lord called Ida Mae and I into the deliverance ministry, we began to share what we had learned with other minister friends. One day there were five of us couples together, and we decided that we would minister deliverance to one another. The men would minister to the men, and the women to the women in a separate room.

We men were in the midst of ministry when we heard the ladies calling for help. They had encountered a demon they couldn't handle. A demon was reacting violently through one of the women, and they couldn't restrain her. So, we five, strong men marched in the room to take charge. The demon in this little lady was stronger than all five of us combined.

19

When we attempted to restrain her and pin her down, she flicked us off like we were flies. We were reminded of the Gadarene demonic whom "no man could bind."

We asked the ladies if they knew the name of the spirit. They replied, "He told us that his name is Itch." I couldn't understand how a spirit of itch could be so strong. "Oh, that couldn't be right," I protested. So, I commanded the spirit to name himself. The demon, speaking through the woman, defiantly asserted, "My name is Itch. I am MR. ITCH!"

After quite a battle the spirit of itch was finally cast out. When I questioned this pastor's wife if she actually had a problem with itching, she said, "Oh, yes!" She was a school teacher, and when she would begin to itch all over her body, she would have to excuse herself from the classroom and go into the teachers' lounge or rest room and scratch herself from head to toe. After the deliverance she had no further problem. Mr. Itch was no longer there!

WATCH OUT FOR YOUR INTERPRETER!

Frank Marzullo and I were ministering in Bogota, Colombia. Our schedule was very packed, and for a week we had ministered three and four services each day. Our interpreter was an elderly pastor. We were all getting very, very tired. I suggested to my interpreter that we place two chairs on the platform and sit down for the next teaching session.

The teaching and interpretation was going very well for awhile, until I said something that my interpreter failed to interpret. I assumed that he didn't understand what I said, so I repeated the sentence. Still no interpretation. I turned to look at him, and he was sitting there sound asleep!

Our first overseas ministry took us to Denmark. Our interpreter was a very dignified brother. As we got up to minister, I turned to my interpreter in jest said, "I expect you to improve on what I say." He was visibly shocked. He replied, "Oh, I can't do that. I will sit down." I grabbed him by the arm and said, "No, don't leave me I need you."

After we finished he turned to me and asked, "Were you teasing?" I told him, "Yes I was just teasing." He shook his head, "I've heard of teasing, but I've never been teased before. People in Denmark don't tease."

Once in Bern, Switzerland and again in Wisla, Poland, the anointed teaching exposed evil spirits in my interpreters. They were so over-powered by the spirits that they were unable to continue. It was necessary to minister deliverance to the interpreters before we could continue with the teaching.

THE HOLY SPIRIT DESCENDED AS A DOVE

I'll never forget the time we were visiting friends in Fort Collins, Colorado. The husband in that home had a respiratory problem and requested prayer. Six of us were in a circle, holding hands and praying for his healing. Suddenly I felt the presence of the Holy Spirit in a most tangible way. It reminded me of Jesus being baptized by John when the Spirit of God descended upon Him like a dove.

Suddenly, over my head I sensed the fluttering of wings, and I felt the Holy Spirit descend upon me like a dove and alight on my head. What an awesome experience!

Then, everyone in the prayer circle broke into laughter. One of the children had left the bird cage open, and the parakeet had flown out and landed on top of my head!

Deaf Mute Delivered from Inherited Curse

Ida Mae and I were ministering in Chattanooga, Tennessee, with a local pastor. It was the very first time we had taught on curses. There was a fourteen-year-old boy in the service who was born totally deaf. His mother brought him forward for prayer. Ida Mae received a word of knowledge that the boy's deafness was the result of a curse due to his mother's involvement in divination.

Ida Mae asked the mother if she indeed was involved in fortune telling. "Yes," she replied. "I was very much into fortune telling before I was saved." So, this was the source of an inherited curse, for the sin of idolatrous divination will produce a curse, *"visiting the iniquity of the fathers upon the children unto the third and fourth generation"* (Exod. 20:5).

The mother had never confessed her involvement in divination as sin, so we ministered to her first, delivering her from the curse. Then, the pastor put his index fingers in the boy's ears, and we commanded the deaf spirit to go. The spirit came out with a cough. He began to hear sound for the first time in his life. Someone began to play a music tape over the church's sound system, and the boy broke into a big smile and nodded his head to the rhythm of the music.

The next day, the mother called to inform the pastor. She was praising the Lord that the boy still had his hearing. He had been mute since birth because he had never heard any sounds. Now he could learn to speak. We all gave thanks and praise to the Lord for this healing miracle.

PART II

the Tales of
Frank Marzullo

THE HOLY SPIRIT KNOWS EVERYTHING

Evelyn and I were ministering in a Deliverance Seminar in Bridgeport, Connecticut some years ago. Attending the seminar were several Italians who did not understand English very well. I spoke to one of them in Italian, trying to explain to her that forgiveness was a must in order to receive deliverance.

I said to the woman, "As an example, here is the way you do it. You must say, I forgive Giovanni, Maria, and Alfredo," picking those names at random.

She looked at me in amazement, and said, "That's right; those are the ones who have caused me so much trouble, Giovanni and Maria, my cousins, and Alfredo, my brother." She asked me, "How did you know?"

I replied, "The Holy Spirit knows everything." Praise God, she did forgive them and receive a good deliverance.

DOING SOMETHING
SHE COULDN'T DO BEFORE

Frank and Ida Mae Hammond and I had just finished our ministry in Cali, Colombia and Pastor Randy MacMillan suggested that we stop at the island of San Andres on our way home. He had a sister church there. San Andres is a beautiful little island near the coast of Nicaragua. We had a wonderful time there, swimming in the blue-green waters of the Gulf of Mexico. It was a very restful place.

The church services were held on a second floor, and when we arrived there the room was packed with people including a woman in a wheel chair. After the sermon, we started to pray for the needs of the people.

I went to the woman in the wheel chair and prayed for her. Then I said to her, "Do something you could not do before." With that word, she struggled to her feet, got up out of the chair, and walked out of the room, down the stairs, and we never saw her anymore. She never came back. She did something she had never done before.

BREAST TUMORS HEALED

We were having a Deliverance Seminar in Carpenter's Home Church in Lakeland, Florida. As is the order of business, I always pray for healing after deliverance, because I believe that the people are more open to healing after the demonic garbage is swept away.

I prayed for a woman who had tumors in her breast. I told her to put her hands on her breast. She did. Then, I put my hands on her hands. I cursed the tumors and commanded them to melt away IN THE NAME OF JESUS.

With that she exclaimed, "They are gone; the tumors have disappeared; praise God!" At testimony time, this woman came up to the platform and testified that, "Frank Marzullo put his hands on my breast, and it is healed." There I was sitting next to my wife and everyone looking at me and laughing at my embarrassment. I explained to my wife that I did not put my hands on the woman's breast, but I did put them on her hands.

The Lord Has a Sense of Humor

In the early days of my ministry, I was a frequent visitor in Good Shepherd Lutheran Church in North Miami, Florida, where Pastor Barber gave me the freedom to pray for people gathered about the altar. One night I was praying for a woman, and the Lord gave me a "word of knowledge" for her. I told her that she had to forgive her husband.

She asked, "Who told you about me?"

I answered, "I don't know you from Adam."

Then, she asked, "How do you know my name?"

I asked her, "What's your name?"

She said, "My last name is Adam."

And I laughed and said, "The Lord sure has a sense of humor." I then explained to her that the Holy Spirit gave me that "word of knowledge."

Casting Out the False Jesus

In deliverance, we've had occasion to test the spirits many times. Jesus said that the devil is a liar and the father of all liars (John 8:44). So, we have to be on guard for the deceiver. Even though we see the manifestations of deliverance, that is, coughing, crying, burping, sneezing, gagging, and the like, we sometimes recheck certain spirits to make sure they are out. The devil can give false manifestations in order to deceive us.

My wife and I were ministering to a woman in our home in Miami some years ago. After about two hours of deliverance, with many manifestations, a sweet voice spoke out of the woman saying, "You don't need to bother anymore, there's no one living here now, they are all gone. This is Jesus speaking."

The woman looked so sweet and had such a lovely smile on her face, she was actually radiant. Suddenly, I felt the inner voice of the Holy Spirit telling me to test the source of the voice that spoke through the woman. I realized, because the scriptures tell me to test the spirits, I was on solid ground.

So, I spoke to that spirit, "You, who calls himself *Jesus*, I bind your power and command you to leave this woman in the name of Jesus Christ of Nazareth, the Son of the living God." I was sure of the Jesus I knew, and I wanted the false *Jesus* to know that he was found out. I had all the authority I needed in that precious name above all names. That false *Jesus* came out gagging and crying. Praise the Lord Jesus Christ.

FRANK'S FAULT

My wife and I were in a bring-your-own-lunch ladies' prayer meeting. After I finished preaching, we all sat down to have lunch. There were about thirty women gathered there. We were sitting at the large dining room table enjoying ourselves with the delicious food and the conversation. Then, Nancy, who was sitting opposite me and who also was very pregnant, pointed to me and then to her large stomach and said in a very loud voice, "Frank Marzullo, this is your fault." My face got very red and everyone was looking at me. Then, Nancy said, "My husband and I could not conceive for ten years, you prayed for me, and this is the result." Then everyone laughed, but my face was still red.

PULLING OUT THE FIERY DARTS

We were ministering at a church in England when a young woman approached us for prayer. She said she had experienced great pain in her back for many years. She had done all, including prayers, fasting, medical attention, but the pain persisted.

In praying for back pain, we often find that a person's one leg is shorter than the other. Because of that, their hip and spine are not perfectly aligned. So, I told her to sit in a chair so that I could measure her legs. I found one leg much shorter than the other.

We prayed and both legs became the same length, but the pain did not go away. I asked her to forgive all who had hurt her. She said that she already had, but would do so again — but the pain was still there.

Then I prayed and asked the Holy Spirit for a "word of knowledge and discerning of spirits." The word that came to me was, "Pull out the fiery dart put there by the devil." I had never done anything like this before, but I obeyed the Holy Spirit.

I said, "Sister, I am going to put my hand on your back and move it down your spine, starting from the nape of your neck. Let me know when I get to the exact point of pain." As I moved my hand, she said, "There." So with a pulling-out motion, I said, "I pull out that fiery dart, in the name of Jesus." With that, the woman gave a loud cry and exclaimed, "It's out! The pain is gone!"

The pain she had for years left her. Praise God! I believe it was a fiery dart, sent by a witch to torment this young woman.

Paul speaks of this in EPHESIANS 6:16,

> "Above all, taking the shield of faith, wherewith ye shall be able
> to quench all the fiery darts of the wicked."

Since that time, the Lord has used my hands for many things, as it says in PSALM 144:1...

> "He teacheth my hands to war, and my fingers to fight..."

BREAKING THE POWER OF VOODOO DOLL CURSES

Another time, in Florence, Italy, we were asked by a priest friend to minister to a man, a high official in a nearby town, and to his wife who was racked with pain in various parts of her body. They had been to many doctors and had even consulted witches in order to get rid of these tormenting pains, but none could help.

They went through the very important step of declaring Jesus Christ as their Lord and Savior. Then, we commanded out spirits of unforgiveness, resentment, all curses, occultism, divination, torment and pain. We anointed her with oil and prayed for her healing, but the pains persisted. I prayed in the Spirit, and the Holy Spirit showed me in a mental picture, a voodoo doll stuck with pins all over its body.

I asked this couple if they had any enemies who might curse them or give them the evil eye. They said they believed that the evil eye was put upon them. It is a common practice in many countries for people to consult witches, witch doctors, or even mediums, to put curses on their enemies by casting an evil eye upon them. Sometimes, a witch would get a doll representing an enemy and would insert pins in various parts of the doll, in order to torment that enemy. The doll might even have some of the enemy's hair, or a picture of that person could be pinned on the doll's body.

The Holy Spirit told me to pull out all those voodoo pins from every part of her body. So, I told my wife to pull out those pins in the name of Jesus. I would indicate where the pins were, and Evelyn would make a pulling-out motion saying, "I pull you out in Jesus' name."

Each time Evelyn did this, the woman would have a painful reaction and then freedom from pain in that area. We pulled those pins out of her ears, her head, her breasts, her side, her back, her rectum, and her female organs. The last were the most painful as they left, but praise God, she was set free of pain.

Another case involving voodoo dolls occurred when we were living in Miami, Florida. A woman called me about her ten-year-old daughter. This little girl (we'll call her Mary) had a beautiful doll, a gift that her godfather bought for her in the West Indies.

One day, she was angry with her sister and after watching a movie about witchcraft and voodoo, she decided to try voodoo on her sister. She called the doll by her sister's name and stuck pins into it. At the same time, her sister who was in school suddenly fell to the floor in agony with pain in various parts of her body.

The school called her mother who went to get her. On returning home, Mary was told about what happened in school. Mary was shocked and frightened to hear what happened to her sister. She confessed that she had stuck pins in that doll and wished harm on her sister. Mary also became frightened when the doll spoke to her and called her by her name. Mary confessed all to her mother, who then called me.

I led Mary to repent of her sins and to receive salvation. She was delivered of all the spirits that came in when she practiced witchcraft. Then, I told Mary that the doll had to be destroyed by fire. She did not want to do this. I gave her a choice — Jesus or the doll. Thank God she chose Jesus. Then I burnt the doll and threw the ashes in the garbage can. Mary learned the bitter lesson that the devil is real and takes advantage of things we think are fun, because we see them in the movies. This doll most likely had a curse put on it by a witch when it was made.

We have to be careful what kind of souvenirs we buy and bring into our home. We are warned by God's word.

> Neither shalt thou bring an abomination into thine house, lest thou be a cursed thing like it: but thou shall utterly detest it, and thou shall utterly abhor it; for it is a cursed thing.
>
> DEUT. 7:26

THE INCUBUS SPIRIT

We lived in Miami, Florida, from 1951 to 1982 in a little house in the Southwest section. When we received the baptism in the Holy Spirit in 1967, we opened our home for prayer meetings. Our Florida room was turned into a church. New Christians of all denominations and races came to our home seeking the knowledge of the Holy Spirit. We learned by "on-the-job" training.

A married couple came one meeting night, and in the middle of our praise and worship, the woman slid off her chair onto the floor. Most of our group thought that she was slain in the Spirit, but the Holy Spirit led me to understand that the demons in her could not stand the praise and worship.

So, I whispered in her ear, "I command you demons to be bound and powerless until this meeting is over."

Then, I had her sit up, and we went on with the meeting. As soon as the meeting came to a close, down she went again. The spirits in her obeyed me to the letter. After we dismissed the others, my wife and I and the woman's husband prayed for a couple of hours. We learned that the girl (we will call her Dorothy) was having a love affair with a familiar spirit, an *incubus spirit*.

Webster's dictionary defines *incubus* as an evil spirit in a male form who tries to sleep with women with whom it seeks sexual intercourse, and a *succubus* spirit is an evil spirit taking a female form who tries to sleep with men. Dorothy had never been able to have intercourse with her husband in three years of their marriage because her vagina was too small, even though she had surgery in an attempt to correct the problem. She was getting comfort from this spirit and had come to love him. She did not realize that the demon had afflicted her with this condition so that she would be unable to have normal relations with her husband and so that he — the spirit — could have her for himself.

After she finally renounced it, we were able to command the incubus spirit to come out of her in the name of Jesus. Then we prayed for her to be healed of her physical impairment. We declared, "We stretch that organ in the name of Jesus," and we made a stretching motion in front of her body. She told us that she felt something stretch within her. A week later, the couple returned and happily told us that for the first time they had normal marital relations. She was healed; praise the Lord. "*He teacheth my hands to war, and my fingers to fight*" (Ps 144:1).

SANTERIA IS OVERCOME BY BLOOD OF JESUS

Another time, I was invited to have a prayer meeting in the home of a Cuban woman named Maria. She asked me to cleanse her house of all evil spirits, including *Santeria* spirits. While we were all praising the Lord with our hands uplifted, in came Maria's mother, Dolores. Maria had told me that her mother was a *Santera*, a Spanish witch. As we raised our hands, so did Dolores. Then I prayed in tongues, and so did she. Dolores imitated everything I did, until the Holy Spirit told me to put the blood of Jesus against her.

I laid my hand upon her forehead and said, "The blood of Jesus is against you." With that, she fell to the floor, and stayed there a long time while we continued to praise the Lord. When Dolores started to get up, I put my hand on her again, pleading the precious blood of Jesus. And again she fell to the floor and remained there a long time.

Then, I was able to minister to Maria and her family God's plan of salvation, without interference from her mother. When we were ready to leave the house, we helped Dolores from the floor. By that time, she realized that she couldn't imitate the blood of Jesus. She met a power that was greater than anything she had. This turned her to accept Jesus Christ as her Lord and Savior. Eventually, she was delivered and now, praise God, she is a faithful member of a Charismatic Lutheran Church in Miami. The precious blood of Jesus is something that the devil cannot imitate. Glory to Jesus Christ!

> And they overcame him by the blood of the Lamb, and by the word of their testimony; and they loved not their lives unto the death.
>
> REV. 12:11

> For the life of the flesh is in the blood.
>
> LEV. 17:11

INHERITED CURSES

> Thou shalt not bow down thyself to them, nor serve them: for I
> the Lord thy God am a jealous God, visiting the iniquity of the
> fathers upon the children unto the third and fourth generation
> of them that hate me.
>
> EXOD. 20:5

We were in our great-grandfather's loins, in our grandfather's loins,
and in our father's loins, before we were born. Therefore, we can inherit
a physical defect — and even a spiritual defect — through our blood
line, *"for the life of the flesh is in the blood"* (LEV. 17:11). We can inherit
evil spirits and curses through our blood line. Many persons who have
received evil spirits in this manner have come to us for ministry.

Susan was a lovely American woman who married an English
minister. They lived near London, England, and I was invited to speak
in their church. They had two children and apparently they were happily
married, and things were going well in their home.

After one of the services, Susan asked for an appointment with my
wife and me. She shared with us that, even though she loved her husband
very much, there were times when she had these terrible urges to take a
knife and mutilate him. I asked about the nationalities in her bloodline.
She told me that one of her ancestors was a Cherokee Indian. The Lord
told me that was the source of her problem.

First, I bound the power of that Cherokee Indian spirit, then I spoke
to that spirit. I said, "You Cherokee Indian spirit, you who likes to
mutilate pale faces, I command you out in the name of Jesus." As soon as I
said this, she came towards me with claw-like hands, yelling, "I'll kill you;
I'll kill you." I put the blood of Jesus between us and kept commanding
that Indian spirit to leave. Suddenly, with a blood-curdling scream, out it
came.

Her husband was a "pale face," and some Indians once killed the white
settlers. That spirit was in her bloodline. That's why she had these feeling
about her pale-faced husband. Praise God for deliverance!

The Pirate Spirit

On the same trip to England, I was conducting a mass deliverance service in a church in Aldershot, not far from London. There, on the front row, was a dainty old lady in her eighties. She was slight in build, wearing white gloves, looking very neat and gentle. She looked like she wouldn't hurt a fly. In the midst of the mass deliverance service, she screamed. Her face took on an ugly appearance. She didn't look like that sweet, dainty lady that came into the meeting. The Lord told me the name of the Spirit.

I said, "You *pirate spirit*, you that wants to cut people in half, I command you out in the name of Jesus."

She looked at me so sweetly and said, "I never cut anyone in half."

I said to her "Yes, but you would like to; wouldn't you?"

She laughed at me and said, "I want to, and I will."

"No you won't," I said. "You are coming out now in the name of Jesus." With a great cough, out it came. I learned later that one of her ancestors had been a pirate.

> If we confess our sins, He is faithful and just to forgive us our sins, and to cleanse us from all unrighteousness.
> 1 John 1:9

> "And his lord, moved with anger, handed him over to the torturers until he should repay all that was owed him. My heavenly Father will also do the same to you, if each of you does not forgive his brother from your heart."
> Matt. 18:34–35 (NASB)

UNCONFESSED SIN

Unconfessed sin opens the door for many evil spirits to enter. Sins such as abortion, attempted abortion, unforgiveness, resentment, envy, covetousness (which is idolatry) are sometimes hidden sins, but they give the devil the right to enter a person nevertheless.

Debra, a member of our prayer group, a woman about fifty years old, called me by phone at 3:30 a.m. one morning.

She cried out, "They are here in my bedroom, a bunch of demon spirits, laughing at me. They are keeping me awake with their noise. I commanded them to go in the name of Jesus, as you taught me, but they won't go."

I told her that if they will not leave after commanding them to go in the name of Jesus, then they have a legal right to be there. I asked her to pray with me and ask the Lord to reveal the legal right that gave entrance to these spirits.

As we prayed, the word "abortion" came to my mind. I asked her if she ever had an abortion. She said that she did many years ago when she was a young girl. I discovered that she never confessed the abortion as sin. I told her to confess it now, and she did. Then I commanded out of her the spirits of *abortion, murder, child sacrifice, lust, fornication,* and all like spirits, and told her to take a deep breath and let it out in the name of Jesus. Then, I told her to command those evil spirits out of her house and tell them not to come back in Jesus' name, and to invite the Holy Spirit into her to take the place of all the evil spirits that were cast out. I also told her to read PSALM 18 out loud in every room of her house. Praise God that those spirits never came back

GETTING TO THE ROOT CAUSES

The Lord taught me to go to the source of abortion in a very unusual way. My brother, Ernest, and I were with a group of sixteen people traveling through Ireland, Northern Ireland, Scotland, and finally into England. One night, we stayed in a castle in middle England. They rented out its rooms to pay for the upkeep of the castle.

My group asked me to bring them a teaching on deliverance. I told them that the best way to teach about deliverance is go through it. So, we had mass deliverance. In the midst of calling out spirits of violence, anger and murder, our song leader, a lovely young woman, started to scream. She suddenly swelled before us like a nine-month pregnant woman.

I commanded that spirit to name itself. It said, "*Baal*." I asked the young woman if she ever had an abortion, and she told me that she had several. After she asked God's forgiveness of the sin of abortion, I commanded out of her: *abortion, child sacrifice, murder*, and the spirits of *Baal* and *Molech*. The Lord was teaching me that I must go to the source of abortion. It's not enough to cut off the branches, but I must go to the root source of these demon spirits. I know that two of the main spirits over the United States are *Baal* and *Molech*. After delivering the young woman, her body returned to it's normal size.

When delivering a person from the spirits of *incest*, I also go to the source, that is, the first time incest is mentioned in the Bible. This is when Lot's two daughters conspired to get their father drunk and had intercourse with him. They gave birth and two nations were formed, Moab and Ammon. The spirit god of Moab was Chemosh, and the spirit god of Ammon was Milcom. When commanding out incest, also cast out the spirits of Chemosh and Milcom.

PLUCKED FROM THE FIRES OF HELL

I was conducting a seminar on Healing and Deliverance at the Community of Faith Church in Bogota, Colombia, South America. My wife, Evelyn, my daughter, Nina, and her husband, Tom Snyder, came with me. My talk was also being broadcast on radio.

I started to bind the powers of darkness that were over the city: the spirits of *witchcraft, devil worship, lust, divination, spiritualism,* and all *occultism,* when all hell broke loose! A woman who was sitting on my left, started to scream and would not stop. The ushers were trying to carry her out of the crowded church. I stopped them and told them to bring the woman to me. I bound every Antichrist spirit within her, in the name of Jesus, and commanded her to sit on the steps of the platform that I was standing on. I told her to obey every command when I started to cast out demons in mass deliverance.

Suddenly, on my right, another commotion started. A young man was pushing people and chairs left and right. He staggered down the aisle towards me with claw-like hands, muttering as he came. Both my wife and I immediately pointed a finger at him and commanded the spirits motivating him to be bound and powerless in the name of Jesus and the power of His blood. He fell right at my feet in front of the speaker's platform and laid there. All this activity was being broadcast on the radio. After order was restored, Tom Snyder helped the young man to his feet and he sat next to him.

I continued on with mass deliverance. When it was over, I started to pray for healing. The woman who was sitting on the step of the platform was delivered of *witchcraft* and many other spirits. She came to me and hugged me with tears flowing down her cheeks. Her countenance was changed, and she looked like a different woman. She had peace.

Nina, Tom and Evelyn ministered to the young man and led him to salvation. He, too, was set free from many spirits. Tom found out that this man was a devil worshipper. Tom told him to burn all books and things pertaining to devil worship. The next night he came back and told us that he did burn everything that he had in his home that was of the devil. That night he received more deliverance. Praise God.

> And the Lord said unto Satan, The Lord rebuke thee, O Satan; even the Lord that hath chosen Jerusalem rebuke thee: is not this a brand plucked out of the fire?"
>
> ZECHARIAH 3:2

Both the young man and the woman were plucked from the fires of hell.

On that last night of the Deliverance Seminar in the Philadelphia Church in Bogota, Colombia, I asked for some testimonies. A very pregnant woman came to the platform. She gave the most blessed testimony I have ever heard.

She said, "Pastor Marzullo, last year I came to you for prayers. I had been married for eight years and could not conceive. I also was heavily involved in witchcraft until I met Jesus as my Lord and Savior. But you said that the Holy Spirit showed you that witchcraft spirits in my female organs were destroying my husband's seed so I could not have children. You commanded those spirits out in Jesus' name and invited the blood of Jesus to come in my female organs and purify them. This is the result," she said as she pointed to her pregnancy.

Praise God, I have been inviting the precious blood of Jesus more and more in my prayers.

WOOPS!

We were ministering in Cali, Colombia, and a young woman came to my wife, Evelyn, and asked for prayer. This woman said that she wanted to get pregnant and so far had been unable to do so. Evelyn prayed for her.

The following year we were again there in Cali. Again, we met that same young woman. Only this time she had a little baby in her arms. She came to Evelyn so that Evelyn could hold the baby and bless him. The woman was very happy and told Evelyn that God had blessed her with this baby and with a husband that she married last week. The father of the babe did not marry her until she could give proof that she could have children. When she had the baby, then he married her. When Evelyn heard the condition, she cried to the Lord and said, "Lord if I had known this before, I do not believe that I would have prayed."

DOG DELIVERED OF BITING SPIRIT

We had a dog named Smokey. Smokey was very protective, and could not stand strangers. He bit five people, and we had to have him in quarantine often. This concerned us greatly. We even thought about putting him to sleep because of it. However, one day, as Evelyn put Smokey on the runner in the back yard, she prayed over him. She commanded the biting demons to leave him in the name of Jesus. With that prayer, Smokey gave a great big yawn, rolled over and went to sleep. He never bit anyone else after that. Praise the Lord, we have authority over the animals in the mighty name of Jesus.

I can do all things through Christ who strengthens me.
PHILIPPIANS 4:13

.

"Behold, I give unto you power to tread on serpents and scorpions, and over all the power of the enemy: and nothing shall by any means hurt you."
LUKE 10:19

TALES OF TWO FRANKS

BIG MISTAKE!

In our early years, my wife, Evelyn, and I learned about deliverance by on-the-job training. In the learning process, we made many mistakes. One of them was a doozy. We had been trying to cast a stubborn spirit out of a woman who came to our prayer meeting, but without success. Then, Evelyn said, "Frank, I'll take on the stubborn spirit, and you can cast it out of me."

As I tried to cast the spirit out of Evelyn, the phone rang. It was my daughter, Cynthia. I told her that I would call her later. As soon as I hung up, Evelyn cried out, "Who was that!" I looked at her. She had her hands on her hips pointing her finger at me in a pose that was just like that stubborn woman. I suddenly realized that I now had two women with stubborn spirits to deal with. I got my Bible. I tried to put my Bible on her back. She ran from me, crawled on her hands and knees went under our baby grand piano, with me with my Bible crawling after her.

I did not know what to do. I yelled, "Jesus help us." And then I again yelled, "You stubborn spirit get out in the name of Jesus." I don't know whether Evelyn coughed or burped, but suddenly she said, "It is gone!"

We learned a big lesson. Never take on another's evil spirit, because if you invite the enemy in, he will come in and bring many more spirits with him.

FRANK HAMMOND TEACHING AVAILABLE ON **VIDEO**

VIDEO STREAMING

Watch video excerpts now at:

www.IMPACTCHRISTIANBOOKS.com/**STREAMING**

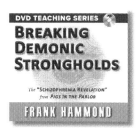

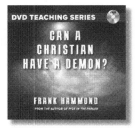

To see Frank Hammond's video library, enter the website shown above - or point your phone's camera at this **QR Code** and click on the link that appears. ⟶

MP3 DOWNLOADS

Frank Hammond's Audio Teachings *Now available for immediate download ... For listening on your computer, phone, tablet or other device.*

www.IMPACTCHRISTIANBOOKS.com/Audio

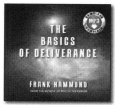
Basics of Deliverance

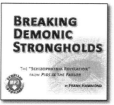
Demonic Strongholds

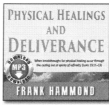
Healing thru Deliverance

Binding the Strongman

Obstacles to Deliverance

Freedom from Soul Ties

Breaking of Curses

Rejection: the Root

The Wiles of the Devil

Deliverance from Self

Mind, Will, Emotions

Spoiling Enemy's House

DELIVERANCE SERIES

FREEDOM SERIES

FAMILY SERIES

END TIME SERIES

RECOGNIZING GOD SERIES

SPIRITUAL MEAT SERIES

HOLY SPIRIT SERIES

Or point your phone's camera at this QR CODE

FRANK HAMMOND BOOKS

PIGS IN THE PARLOR
9780892280278

A handbook for deliverance from demons and spiritual oppression, patterned after the ministry of Jesus Christ. With over *1 million copies in print* worldwide, and translated into more than a dozen languages, *Pigs in the Parlor* remains the authoritative book on the subject of deliverance.

STUDY GUIDE: PIGS IN THE PARLOR
9780892281992

Designed as a study tool for either individuals or groups, this guide will enable you to diagnose your personal deliverance needs, walk you through the process of becoming free, and equip you to set others free from demonic torment. Includes questions and answers on a chapter-by-chapter basis as well as new information to further your knowledge of deliverance.

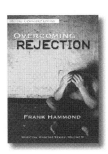

OVERCOMING REJECTION
9780892284290

Rejection is one of the most common wounds, but it can occur at any stage in life. The good news is that the Spirit of the Lord seeks to restore our soul (Ps 23), and to bring forth a confidence in who we truly are in Jesus. At this moment, your Savior wants you to be stable in His love. *It is time to break this stronghold in your life!*

THE BREAKING OF CURSES
9780892281091

The Bible refers to curses over 230 times, and seventy sins that cause curses are listed in Scripture. The key to understand their power is to know that behind every curse there is a demon with some legal right to enact the curse. Curses are just as real today as they were in Biblical times.

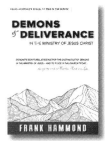

DEMONS & DELIVERANCE IN THE MINISTRY OF JESUS

As a sequel to Pigs in the Parlor, Frank Hammond sets forth guiding principles from Scripture and the ministry of Jesus for confronting demons and delivering the oppressed. Studying the methods of Jesus in the Bible helps us avoid unhealthy, unbiblical and even occult practices from getting a foothold in the deliverance ministry.
9780892280018

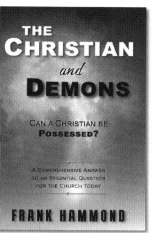

CAN A CHRISTIAN BE POSSESSED?
LIKE IN THE MOVIES?

Most Christians are sensitive enough to not get their theology from Hollywood. And yet in this particular area, when the subject of demons is mentioned, most people immediately think of movies and television portrayals of demons and deliverance. This is partly why this powerful ministry of Jesus has become one of the most challenging and controversial issues in the Body of Christ today. The uncertainty surrounding this issue creates an obstacle to the greater move of the Holy Spirit taking place on earth. Frank Hammond answers pressing questions about the deliverance ministry, and whether it applies to Christians today...

HOW CAN A CHRISTIAN, WITH THE HOLY SPIRIT DWELLING IN HIM, HAVE A DEMON?

HOW DOES DEMONIC ACTIVITY COMPARE TO WHAT I HAVE SEEN ON TV OR IN MOVIES?

ISN'T THIS A MINISTRY FOR REALLY MESSED UP PEOPLE, BEFORE THEY ACCEPT JESUS?

AREN'T MOST OF MY PROBLEMS PHYSICAL, NOT SPIRITUAL?

DOES THE BIBLE ACTUALLY SAY CHRISTIANS CAN BE POSSESSED?

PHYSICAL HEALINGS THRU DELIVERANCE

When breakthroughs for physical healing occur through the casting out of spirits of infirmity... In our deliverance ministry over the years, we have seen many physical healings result from the casting out of evil spirits. We have recorded a number of these miraculous testimonies in this book (including crippling, curvature of the spine, deafness and more). This teaching identifies the most common spiritual roots of sickness, and we offer a prayer of deliverance from the enemy's harassment against our physical bodies.

BOOKS THAT MINISTER TO CHILDREN & FAMILIES

DELIVERANCE FOR CHILDREN & TEENS

A practical handbook for ministering deliverance to children. Lear
simple, surprising truths: the easiest of all ministry is to sma
children, Discipline is a basic form of spiritual warfare, Demon
problems can come through heredity or experience. *Informatio
and cases collected in over 30 years of ministry to families.*

9780892280346

THE LITTLE SKUNK:
A CHILDREN'S GUIDE TO DELIVERANCE

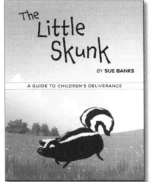

A skunk is trapped inside a home and children are faced with the question of how
to get it out. This is a children's story that can be read by a parent to a child as a way
of introducing the subject of deliverance without fear. Written with color illustrations
to accompany the story, and assistance at the end to help parents pray with a child.
DELIVERANCE NEED NOT BE FRIGHTENING IF PROPERLY PRESENTED.

9780892280780

A MANUAL FOR CHILDREN'S DELIVERANCE

Deliverance truths, in simple terms, for setting children free from
fears, torments and destructive behavior. Children today are
bombarded more than any time in history with satanic influences.
There is a war being waged for their imaginations and for their
souls. Frank and Ida Mae Hammond draw upon their rich
experience in dealing with children and in helping them receive
the freedom purchased for them through the cross of Jesus Christ.

OTHER FRANK HAMMOND BOOKS

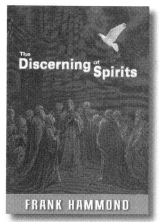

9780892283682

THE DISCERNING OF SPIRITS

We are equipped by God for spiritual warfare through the gifts of the Holy Spirit mentioned in 1 Corinthians 12. God has said that these are the channels through which His power will flow, the avenues through which His Holy Spirit will operate. Chief among these gifts for the ministry of deliverance is the gift of the discerning of spirits. Frank Hammond explains the application of this gift to the believer, and provides examples of how it has worked in his own ministry.

SPIRITUAL WARFARE FOR LOST LOVED ONES

Free will is the greatest gift mankind has been given by their Creator. God does not drive us to Himself, but leads us gently with cords of lovingkindness. Through spiritual warfare, intercessory prayer and the ministry of love, we are able to create the best possible environment around a loved one to come to know Jesus. Frank Hammond says, "Don't let your family or friends go without resistance. Get in the spiritual battle, fight for your loves ones!"

9780892283842

POLTERGEISTS - DEMONS IN THE HOME

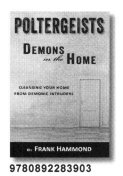

9780892283903

Do you, or someone you know, have demonic spirits in the home? Are you thrust out of sleep by banging doors, the sound of footsteps, lights going on and off? Do you see mysterious shadows on the wall or creatures at the foot of your bed? If so, there is good news for you. Your house can be cleansed! Just as the inside man can be swept clean of demonic spirits, so too can a house or a dwelling be swept clean from the evil presence and harassment of demonic spirits.

LEARN THE BLESSINGS OF GOOD SOUL-TIES & HOW TO BREAK UNGODLY TIES...

"Here at last is a thorough and theologically sound treatment of a little understood subject"   - from the Foreword by **Frank Hammond**

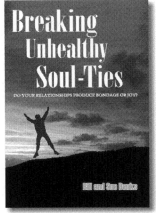

9780892281398

BREAKING UNHEALTHY SOUL-TIES
by Bill & Sue Banks

Today's world has conditioned us to give our soul to another without thought of the long-term consequences. Many are tired and weary from heartbreak, and from living under the power of the demonic. God desires to restore our souls that we might be able to seek Him with our whole spirit, soul and body. Unhealthy soul-ties seek to prevent this, through the control of one individual over another.

STUDY GUIDE:
BREAKING UNHEALTHY SOUL-TIES
BY BILL & SUE BANKS

9780892282043

9780892284351

SOUL TIES

Frank Hammond's booklet on soul ties. Good soul ties include marriage, friendship, parent to child, and between sincere Christians. Bad soul ties include those formed from fornication, evil companions, perverted family ties, with the dead, and demonic ties through the Church.

AUDIO CD: FREEDOM FROM DEMONIC SOUL TIES

Frank Hammond teaches on healthy and unhealthy soul ties in this Audio series, including an extended ministry time at the end for breaking demonic ties to the soul.

9780892283613 CD

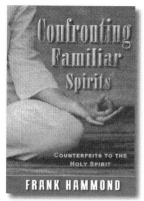

9780892280179

CONFRONTING FAMILIAR SPIRITS

A person can form a close relationship with an evil spirit, willfully or through ignorance, for the purposes of knowledge, financial gain, promotion or power. When a person forms a relationship with an unclean spirit, he or she "has a familiar spirit" or what can be called a *"spirit guide."* Familiar spirits operate as counterfeits to the gifts of the Holy Spirit. These counterfeit spirits are found throughout society, even at times within the Church. The Holy Spirit offers all we need in terms of access to the spiritual realm

9780892282036

OBSTACLES TO DELIVERANCE

WHY DELIVERANCE SOMETIMES FAILS

Why does deliverance sometimes fail? This is, in essence, the same question raised by Jesus' first disciples, when they were unable to cast out a spirit of epilepsy from a young child. Jesus gave a multi-part answer which leads us to take into account the strength of the spirit confronted and the strategy of warfare employed.

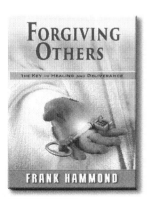

9780892280766

FORGIVING OTHERS:
THE KEY TO HEALING & DELIVERANCE

Unforgiveness is an obstacle to our walk with Jesus, and can be a roadblock to the deliverance and freedom of our souls. Frank Hammond explains the spiritual truths in the necessity of forgiveness and the blessings of freedom which result.

9780892283859

PRAISE: A WEAPON OF DELIVERANCE

Praise is a mighty weapon and the enemy knows it. He detests it because he fears it. Why? Because it is such a powerful force that destroys his grip on the spiritual atmosphere around us. *Praise clears the air*. What happened when David began to play on his harp and sing praise to his God? The evil spirit departed from King Saul. As you praise the Lord, things begin to happen in the unseen realm. A demon cannot exist in that atmosphere — he simply cannot function.

9780892281602

THE PERILS OF PASSIVITY

There is a purpose in God for each of us - and it is not passivity! Passivity is a foe to all believers in Christ – it can even hinder our intimacy with Jesus. Without an aggressive stance against the enemy, we can easily fall into passivity, and our service to the Lord can be limited. We lose our spiritual sharpness, which as Paul says, is necessary for us to be "sober, alert and diligent."

9780892281046

THE SAINTS AT WAR

There is a war on for your community, your city and your nation. Christians are in conflict with demons and territorial spirits. This is nothing new: the prophet Daniel confronted the "prince of Persia" when interceding for the captive people of God. Thanks to the power of the Holy Spirit, now you and I can be involved in this fight to change the course of history.

9780892280322

DELIVERANCE FROM FAT & EATING DISORDERS

Help for those who have been unable to lose weight or have struggled with eating disorders. Learn about possible spiritual roots and spiritual issues related to food. This is an eye-opening look at the role food can play as a substitute for stability in the love of Jesus. Bill Banks reveals dozens of spiritual reasons for unnatural weight gain, as well as eating disorders like Bulimia and Anorexia.

... ON DEFEATING SEXUAL STRONGHOLDS

REPERCUSSIONS FROM SEXUAL SINS 0892282053

The sexual revolution has entered the Church. Promiscuity, nudity, pornography and obscenities are now commonplace in our society. The inevitable consequence of defilement is the loss of fellowship with a holy God. But we can break free from the bondage of sexual addiction! Hope lies in the deliverance ministry of Jesus and the fruit of the Holy Spirit; these will produce **strong hearts** & **sound minds.**

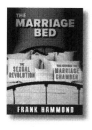

THE MARRIAGE BED 0892281863

The sexual revolution entered the marriage chamber. What is God-ordained activity and what is demonic-inspired activity in the bedroom? God does not change, nor does His standard of what love is. This booklet clears away confusion from the Biblical perspective and explains how to *avoid perverse demonic activity in a home.*

MINISTERING TO ABORTION'S AFTERMATH 0892281863

The world has sold us a lie: a life without consequences. As a result, millions of women have had abortions. Those who are tormented by pain and regret of this decision have access to the throne of God to receive His mercy and love. They also have access to the mighty delivering power of His Holy Spirit. Read a dozen accounts of women who have found freedom from the burdens associated with abortions. Learn how their triumph can be yours!

Impact Christian Books

Website: WWW.IMPACTCHRISTIANBOOKS.COM

Phone Order Line: (314)-822-3309

Address: IMPACT CHRISTIAN BOOKS
332 Leffingwell Ave. #101
Kirkwood, MO 63122 USA

Made in the USA
Middletown, DE
27 August 2024

59874726R00029